Table of Contents

Congratulations Graduate! Now What?

First of all, congratulations on your college degree. All those hours studying your chosen craft of marketing has finally paid off. You've celebrated your accomplishment, cleaned up your apartment, and have said your goodbyes.

What's your next step?

If you're reading this, you are one of the many three to four million college graduates this year majoring in marketing, which in the real world, is a lot of different things. When many of you land jobs, you will plan events, while others of you will get to use Facebook and Twitter every day -- and that's only the tip of the iceberg.

You've also decided that you want to live in the San Francisco Bay Area, one of the most beautiful places in the world with 300 days of sun per year, a thriving technology economy, and unfortunately high rent. You need a job, and you need it fast. Where will you go? What will you do?

Will you do what your alma mater's career center told you? Chances are they have a job board they've encouraged you to use exclusively or they gave you a one-sheet upon graduation that pointed you to job sites like Monster, CareerBuilder, and Indeed.

According to the *Wall Street Journal*, 90% of jobs are filled through employee referrals. In short, if you aren't well connected, you're not doing yourself a disservice. If you're combing job boards for your dream job, the likelihood of finding one is incredibly low.

So what do you do?

If you're me, you hoped for the best when you graduated. My college didn't teach me the importance of networking off campus -- and yours probably didn't either. When that was mixed in with the worst recession in 70 years, I was as unprepared as I could be. I had no idea which resources were available to me, who I should talk to, or where to go. In the end, I ended up having to feel my way through the dark before I found the light. Nobody deserves to feel this way.

I've written this book for you because I don't think anyone should have to go through my experience. I believe that everyone deserves an opportunity to thrive and find something so their college degree can mean more than just a piece of paper. Even if they majored in something completely unrelated to marketing, they deserve to find something meaningful. I'm committed to closing the gap in the job market and have helped people find work at companies like Google, GoPro, and eBay. I can help you do the same.

So if you're ready, join me and read through the rest of this book.

An Introduction to Networking in the San Francisco Bay Area

Chances are you know what networking is, but you're unsure of how it actually works. Maybe you've even attended a networking event yourself, and found the experience to be less than desirable as you saw business cards being thrown around, and 5-second introductions that leave no lasting impressions.

Thankfully, that's not networking.

Real networking focuses on people. As with having any conversation, the ability to listen in a conversation as opposed to speaking someone else's ears off is paramount. If anything, any opportunity you have to talk to people, whether it's a party or in line outside of a coffee shop can be considered networking. In this chapter, we'll discuss the steps you can take to find the networking event that will help you find work

The Art of Active Networking, San Francisco

Finding Networking Events

The first task of going to a networking event is finding one. There are many events to sift through online, and you can either go by individual event or a directory listing like meetup.com or eventbrite.com.

Networking Basics

As a new graduate you're coming into a whole new world. Unlike the world of academics, this one is not governed by tests and homework, but rather by the relationships you make with others. **Quite simply, networking is not about who you know or even what you know, but who knows you.** The more you're able to put yourself out there, create a personal brand, and optimize your audience, the better chances you'll have at landing a job that suits your interests. Since you majored in marketing, what's a better time to make yourself well known by turning your job search into a marketing case study?

Here are some tips on networking basics:

1. **Dress to impress:** You only get one chance to make a first impression, so make sure that impression is memorable. For men, a dress shirt, dress shoes, and dress pants with a belt are fine for most San Francisco Bay Area events. Leave the tie at home unless the event description says so -- you'll be overdressing by wearing one. For women, wearing a neutrally colored pencil skirt or a blouse is appropriate. Go light on the perfume and bring an extra pair of comfortable shoes if you find yourself doing a lot of working. For both genders, adding a scarf may also be appropriate depending on the severity of the weather.

2. **Know your audience**: Marketing is a wide subject. There's digital, social, paid, content, event, video, communications, PR, email, and so much more. Though you'll find professionals in each of these areas at events you go to, the more specific you get, the better results you will have.

3. **Know your why**: The San Francisco Bay Area is a large place. If you live in San Jose and want to go to an event in San Francisco, know what you are going to get out of it. Driving from the South Bay to the City is at least 45 minutes during rush hour, and that does not include parking or BART. Before you go, you should know why you are attending a particular event. This can be to find a new job, meet new people in the industry, or learn some new content that will help you in your career.

4. **Bring your business cards**: You'll not only want to get in front of other people, but you'll want to be memorable as well. Before you go to any event, don't forget to purchase business cards. You can do so at a printing store like Kinko's or online at sites like Vistaprint or Moo.

5. **Leave the resume at home**: The people you network with are not going to want to see your resume, nor have time to read it. The business card should be enough. If they are interested in learning more, you'll be asked for your resume. Bringing your resume to a networking event can come across as desperate.

Here are some tips to master the conversation:

1. **Come from value**: Your first instinct to ask each and every person you meet what they do. This is natural, but also the wrong way to do it because it's what everyone else in the room will be asking as well. Your job as a networker is come from value, and that means asking why the person showed up or how you can help them. Most people attend networking events for themselves and not for other people

2. **Listen more than you speak**: Human beings were made to listen. Actively seek out what the other person is looking for and see if you can help them. If anything, you've already met a few other people and might know who to point this person to in case you can't help.

3. **Be respectful of the diversity**: The San Francisco Bay Area is a diverse region with numerous cultures, viewpoints, and people. On any given night you may meet someone who practices a different faith, shares a different political value, or is

a transplant from another part of the world. When engaging in conversation, keep your interactions conservative. Touching should only occur in shaking the other person's hand.

4. **Don't sell - tell your story instead**: It's natural to also think that networking events are where you sell. While everyone expects to be sold, it's important to stay in the area of value and listen. Straight selling might feel like it's helping you, but you're honestly turning people off more than anything else. Instead, tell a story of what you want, what you are looking for, and how this person you're telling your story to can join in the journey.

5. **Maintain eye contact**: Eye contact is doubly important. You show the person you are networking with that you are paying attention to what they have to say.

6. **Give everyone the time they deserve**: You might meet someone who does not get you closer to your goals. While you may be tempted to move on quickly, the better path is to get the most out of each conversation you have with others. You never know who others know.

As you move around the room throughout the night, you'll have positive conversations as well as negative ones where you feel like there could be more to be desired. In a networking context, this is perfectly acceptable and expected since a variety of people will show up.

When the event reaches its conclusion, your task is still not done. While you may have given out business cards, it's natural to expect that others will find and add you on LinkedIn or send you an email. This is not the time to place those business cards in a rubber band and put them away, but rather to follow up:

1. **Follow up promptly**: When you return home from the event, follow up with the people you met. This can be in the form of email, a phone call, a Facebook or LinkedIn add, or a combination of them all. The longer you wait; the sooner you will forget why you met them in the first place.

2. **Create a call to action**: In marketing, a call to action encourages the other party to do something to further the relationship. In a networking conversation, this is anything from meeting for coffee to getting lunch to a phone call. The best business is still face-to-face.

3. **Continue referring**: Even though the networking might be over, continuing to add value is key. Whether this is sending more business to someone you met or sharing an article that you think another person might like, doing so keeps you on their radar so they know to do the same when they reach out to you.

With this advice in hand, you're ready to go and network in the vast reaches of the San Francisco Bay Area. In our next chapter, we'll cover off on some personal branding tips so your networking efforts will pay off even better before and after you step into the event space.

An Introduction to Personal Branding in the San Francisco Bay Area

Ask any marketing professional you meet in the San Francisco Bay Area and they will tell you two things:

1. It's a very small world
2. A personal brand is key to success

The concept of a personal brand was no doubt introduced to you while you were still in school. The practice is defined as the act of marketing oneself and their career in equivalence to how a company would. Since personal brand falls in the line of marketing, becoming good at selling yourself is literally the ticket to industry survival.

This chapter will cover the basics of personal branding from an online and offline perspective while encouraging their merging for a cohesive and consistent professional networking experience.

The Basics

Like a company brand, a personal brand is all about the messaging, feeling, and direction. As the CEO of your own life, developing a personal brand is akin to creating and managing a career-long marketing campaign with the intention of increasing awareness for your professional intents.

Having the right branding elements matters.

Thus, crafting a personal brand comes down to several basics:

1. **A thoughtful message**: Every single brand takes a stand for a world they believe in. For an individual,

this thoughtful message may require you to consider your strengths and beliefs, whether it's focusing on a focused skill like creating content or an industry like cloud computing.

2. **A commitment**: Messages without action don't go very far. Deciding how you will commit to the message you've placed out there will allow your followers to hold you accountable.

3. **An offer**: Finally, a personal brand provides an offer. This offer is not a strict sales pitch but instead tells the recipient how you show up in their lives. For example, someone could offer to share information and be a thought leader around the emergence of Snapchat as a viable marketing avenue.

Now that we have the basics down, let's take a look at how personal branding shows up in online and in-person.

Online Personal Branding

Social networks have offered the opportunity for individuals to connect with just about anyone across the world. Whether it's rich interactive media like videos and status updates on Facebook or simpler 140 character messages on Twitter, each offer an opportunity to share a message, put yourself out there, and communicate what you are looking for. As stated in the previous chapter, **it's not who you know or what you know, it's who knows you**. The more you are top of mind for other individuals, the more they might be willing to find ways to help you.

Though social networks have gotten noisier, it's also important to control your messaging. Personal branding does not mean tying your Twitter account to your Facebook and having updates pushed every 30 minutes so you stay at the top of someone's news feed. In fact, doing just that will likely get you hidden or blocked.

In the San Francisco Bay Area, personal branding is especially used by major corporate executives to share ideas and concepts. If you do your work and enter into the right circles, the next person you network with might just recognize you.

Consider the following online social media personal branding tips instead:

1. **LinkedIn:** LinkedIn is the most important social network, especially for connecting with those you just met at a networking event. It's also where employers go when they are hunting for qualified candidates. When updating your LinkedIn profile, consider doing the following:
   a. **Updating your profile summary** – this is what most people see first. Mention your intentions for your career and how people can get in touch.
   b. **Filling out your job history**: Simply placing your job title and company is not enough. Since your LinkedIn is a breathing, living, webpage, filling out the relevant portions will let employers see what you've accomplished.
   c. **Filling out your education**: This is also important, especially if you have certifications. Many employers look for potential candidates with specific certifications and having them on your LinkedIn is very helpful.
   d. **Your profile picture**: A brand needs to have an identity. Don't leave this part blank.
   e. **Use LinkedIn Pulse (or start your own blog)**: LinkedIn launched Pulse a few years back to give users the opportunity to share

their thoughts on professional topics. Using Pulse regularly will help drive traffic to your content while helping you work towards your status as a thought leader. It's also a great way to become a better writer.

2. **Twitter**: Known as the network that allows individuals to communicate in 140 characters or less, Twitter is the perfect spot to get to know others and share your expertise and knowledge. When updating your Twitter profile, consider doing the following:
   a. **Refining your bio**: For many people, the bio is the first place people go when landing on your Twitter account. You can indicate your school, major, career intention, and other identifiers. Hashtag accordingly.
   b. **Be mindful of what you share**: Things get lost in the Twitter timeline, but what you share will be seen forever. Make sure you're sharing what you want other people to know you for.
   c. **Engage in the conversation**: Unlike LinkedIn and Facebook, Twitter removes the barrier to engagement in conversation. Get to know others by tweeting at them, commenting on something they shared, or simply thanking them. You never know where that might go.

3. **Facebook**: Many of you know Facebook as the social network you hopped on because your friends were doing so. Over the years, the site has become a place where employers will also comb to make sure you are fit to be hired. When updating your Facebook profile, consider the following:
   a. **Clean up the partying**: We've all had a crazy night or three in college, but the professional world is all business. Delete or

change the privacy to any photos you don't want a prospective employer to see.

b. **Create lists**: One of the niftier benefits of Facebook is the ability to create lists for your friends. This allows you to deliver status updates to a specific group of people. If your colleagues or friends you network with become a part of you network, this is an easy way to make sure they don't see what they don't need to.

In addition to social networks, purchasing your own domain name for a portfolio is also encouraged. Alternatively, you can also consider using platforms like **Medium** or **Strikingly** to create content on already-existing and scaled up platforms. By creating more content, you will be easily searchable.

Finally, how you conduct your personal brand online is a job in itself. Consistently creating content, adding value to others, and engaging in conversations will create the momentum needed to get the right type of attention.

With these tactics in place, you'll be ready to start building your brand online and create opportunity at every turn. In our next section, we discuss how that connects with what you do at the actual event.

Offline Personal Branding

Similar to its online cousin, offline personal branding also emphasizes the importance of capturing attention, but in a live setting. In many cases, you'll be meeting people for anywhere between 60 seconds to three minutes and offering up the right information matters the most. Even if you've done some pre-networking by reaching out to attendees online before they go to the event, you still need put your best self out there. Check out our section on networking above for the main ideas.

Marketing Networking Events, A-Z

Over the next few pages we share a listing of marketing networking events we've attended throughout the years in the San Francisco Bay Area. The costs, people, and time spent at these events differs from month to month, but we believe they are a good sampling to get your intentions started.

If you're an event planner and want to be considered in future editions, send me an email at albert@albertslist.org.

Albert's List Happy Hour, Fall 2015

The Art of Active Networking

Where/When: San Francisco, select Mondays once or twice a month from 6:30 - 9:30 p.m.

What: The Art of Active Networking was started by Mark E. Sackett in 2009 because he saw everyone struggling and lost in their networking endeavors. Mark started the event which now attracts between 80 to 120 attendees per month. At this particular event, Mark gives everyone the chance to stand up and explain what they are looking for in 30 seconds or less, giving everyone a voice. Since the event's founding, Mark has held the event in Vancouver, Los Angeles, New York City, Kansas City, and Orange County.

Why the Marketer Should Attend: Mark is the ultimate entrepreneur, founding 13 different companies across different industries and is worth the price of admission. What sets this event apart from others in San Francisco is a community that is engaged and ready to help, in addition to the resources that Mark provides through his Facebook and LinkedIn groups. For the new graduate, this event is a perfect opportunity to learn how to network properly, meet major players in San Francisco, and go home with contacts willing and ready to help.

Cost: $20 online, $30 at the door

Link: http://www.theartofactivenetworking.com

Albert's Job Listings & Referrals (Facebook Group)

Where/When: Check the Facebook Group

What: Albert's Job Listings and Referrals is a Facebook group for Albert's List, a job search marketplace focused on jobs in the Bay Area and Southern California. In this group, recruiters, job seekers, and employees with the power of referral post their jobs as well as upcoming networking events in marketing and other industries.

Why the Marketer Should Attend: New graduates will find fellow graduates in this group, as the average age is fairly young. There are a lot of marketing jobs available in the group, including contract opportunities at Google. Group members are known to be helpful in assisting others in their hunt for resources, jobs, and contacts.

Cost: Free, extra services available for purchase

Link:
http://www.facebook.com/groups/findyournextopportunity and http://www.albertslist.org

Business Marketing Association (BMA) - NorCal

Where/When: Various locations throughout the Bay Area, Various times during the month

What: BMA, short for Business Marketing Association, was a professional association founded in 1938 by marketing and business professionals. Members tend to be of all career levels, ranging from those just starting out to the most seasoned of executives.

Why the Marketer Should Attend: Silicon Valley at its heart is all about the B2B marketplace, and BMA covers this from the collaborative economy to the noise of modern marketing channels. Attendees get a chance to listen to fellow industry professionals speak about the relevant issues that govern the B2B marketing landscape and go home with fresh insights and strategies.

Cost: Varies per event, a yearly membership fee is also collected.

Link: http://www.norcalbma.org

Community Management (CMX) Hub

Where/When: Online, with conferences yearly around the United States

What: For new graduates who aspire to become community managers, CMX Hub needs to be on their list of places to be. In this community, community managers help each other navigate the rough and tumble world of the fairly new career track of community manager.

Why the Marketer Should Attend: Community managers are all about community, and CMX Hub makes that possible. When embarking on any professional journey, finding the people who make the experience more positive and understanding is always a good thing.

Cost: Free, with a cost to attend conferences

Link: https://www.facebook.com/groups/cmxhub/

EPIC - Young Professionals Network (Palo Alto)

Where/When: Locations vary, but most are held within the Palo Alto to Mountain View metro.

What: Epic stands for "Emerging Professionals in Commerce", and is a program of Palo Alto Chamber of Commerce. The purpose of the group is for the next generation of business leaders to network, gain leadership insight, and get involved in the Palo Alto community.

Why the Marketer Should Attend: Young professionals struggling to find a network after graduating from college will find EPIC to be a very helpful resource. Because their orientation is towards a younger demographic, attendees will be able to connect with like-minded individuals. While not marketing specific, one may be able to find someone who works in marketing at a similar level of experience. This is known to be one of the better young professional networks due to its proximity to Palo Alto.

Cost: Varies per event

Link: http://epicpaloalto.com/

First Thursdays Silicon Valley

Where/When: Various locations around the Bay Area, weekly basis

What: A place for marketing professionals to discuss emerging strategies and trends, as well as a place for all of those interested to get to know more. The group discusses new digital, community and media tools and strategies to launch successful Go-To-Market plans, enhance participation on various communities, and increase customer engagement.

Why the Marketer Should Attend: Marketing is a very transient topic, and staying in the know is half the battle. First Thursdays Silicon Valley offers the opportunity to stay up to speed on trends like digital, social media, mobile marketing, and more, while providing a consistent community that gets together on a regular basis.

Cost: Varies per event

Link: http://www.meetup.com/FirstThursdaysSiliconValley/

#JobHuntChat

Where/When: On Twitter, Monday evenings at 7 p.m., off on holidays

What: Twitter, under the hashtag #jobhuntchat.

Why the Marketer Should Attend: As far as Twitter chats go, this one is very helpful. Moderators ask a series of six questions around a job hunt topic like resumes, cover letters, interviews, and more, often with great responses. Towards the end, members have a chance to share their LinkedIn profiles and meet fellow professionals from around the United States. Recruiters will show up on occasion as well.

Cost: Free

Link: Just sign into Twitter 5 minutes before 7 every Monday evening. Stream the Twitter chat on a site like www.tweetchat.com.

Jewish Vocational Services (JVS)

Where/When: San Francisco, East Bay, and Palo Alto on a weekly basis. Check calendar for dates and times

What: JVS transforms lives by helping people build skills and find jobs to achieve self-sufficiency. JVS's training, programs and resources have helped Bay Area job seekers to build in-demand skills and confidence, make connections and find jobs for 40 years. The majority of their services take place in our Financial District office, with some workshops and services taking place in the East Bay, as well as the North and South Peninsula.

Why the Marketer Should Attend: Like some of the organizations on this list, JVS isn't so much marketing focused as it is resource and tactical focused. Job seekers will find a plethora of events at JVS offices where they can learn everything from Microsoft Excel to editing their cover letter to creating a LinkedIn profile. The services are free as well with personal support, so those who take advantage are getting a bang for their buck.

Cost: Free

Link: http://www.jvs.org/

Network After Work

Where/When: Monthly with varying locations in the Silicon Valley and San Francisco areas.

What: Network After Work describes itself as the premiere networking event. Held nationally in all major cities, this event attracts hundreds of professionals who converge to meet each other.

Why the Marketer Should Attend: For the new graduate, this event is great due to the variety of attendees. Everyone from financial advisors to salespeople to functional professionals shows up to this event and creates an environment to having productive conversations. If, however you do know what you want to do in the marketing space, then this event is something you should skip.

Cost: $12 online, $20 at the door.

Link: http://www.networkafterwork.com

Public Relations Society of America (PRSA)

Where/When: Every second Thursday of the month as well as variable content-based events. Silicon Valley and San Francisco both have chapters which meet in various areas in their respective regions.

What: The Public Relations Society of America is a professional network geared at public relations, marketing, and agency professionals.

Why the Marketer Should Attend: If you're interested in working in public relations, marketing, or at a news wire type company, PRSA is the place to be. The goldmine of PRSA is Second Thursday, which is a free opportunity for the marketer to meet fellow industry professionals as well as hear about open job listings and volunteer opportunities. Recruiters show up at every event as well looking to help fill the rolls at local agencies hunting for talent to help their clients on their next campaign.

Cost: Second Thursday is free, while content events have a fee.

Link: http://www.prsasf.org

General Assembly

Where/When: San Francisco and surrounds, usually in the evenings. Courses are more immersive and can be flexible depending on schedule

What: Established in early 2011 as an innovative community in New York City for entrepreneurs and startup companies, General Assembly is an educational institution that transforms thinkers into creators through education in technology, business and design at fourteen campuses across four continents. Programs offered include full-time immersive programs, long-form courses, and classes and workshops on the most relevant skills of the 21st century – from web development and user experience design, to business fundamentals, to data science, to product management and digital marketing.

Why the Marketer Should Attend: What school teaches and what the real world is looking for often comes out to two different things. General Assembly can both enhance or complement the education already learned by giving attendees a chance to be more relevant in the working world. Marketers might be most interested in courses around digital marketing, content marketing, and social media.

Cost: Varies per individual event. Introduction events are free while taking an education course will cost some money.

Link: https://generalassemb.ly/san-francisco

International Association of Business Communicators (IABC)

Where/When: Monthly, around the San Francisco Bay Area

What: International Association of Business Communicators is a global network of communications professionals. The associations themselves host conversations with communications professionals as well as networking events.

Why the Marketer Should Attend: Attending an IABC event means getting a targeted audience, since many attendees tend to be in the communications field. Marketers should attend for the chance at professional development, mentorship, and the opportunity to build their career through connections and education.

Cost: Yearly fee for membership and separate cost for each event

Link: http://www.sviabc.com

San Francisco American Marketing Association (SFAMA)

Where/When: Around the San Francisco Bay Area, timings vary

What: The American Marketing Association, founded in 1937, is a professional association for marketing professionals with more than 30,000 members across 76 professional and 250 student chapters across the United States.

Why the Marketer Should Attend: Marketing is a dynamic career, and joining an association to hear about the latest is important. Both SFAMA and SVAMA hold weekly webinars as well as in-person gatherings where professionals can make contacts and network. Events are also held at marketing agencies and notable companies, giving job seekers the chance to meet recruiters and employees of these firms.

Cost: Free and paid events. Yearly membership fee and separate fee per event

Link: http://www.sfama.org

San Francisco Online Advertisers and Publishers

Where/When: San Francisco, at various companies and venues

What: SFAdPub is a monthly event that brings together the San Francisco Bay Area's Online Advertising community. Each month they select a relevant topic that we focus on as a group and usually bring in a local expert (or experts) to present, with an opportunity to network with speakers or attendees after the event.

Why the Marketer Should Attend: For marketers who want to start or augment a career in the online space, SF Online Advertisers and Publishers is perfect. The group covers a variety of topics from CRM usage to app monetization, and SEO.

Cost: Free

Link: http://www.meetup.com/sfadpub/

Silicon Valley Startup, Idea to IPO

Where/When: San Jose to San Francisco, daily

What: Idea to IPO is an organization focused on promoting the spirit of entrepreneurship through daily events, many of which cover topics around funding, marketing, valuations, business strategy, and much more. Lectures are covered by various industry thought leaders.

Why the Marketer Should Attend: Startup culture is heavy in Silicon Valley and the San Francisco Bay Area and many entrepreneurs are always on the hunt for new ways to growth hack their idea into the mainstream. For the recent graduate, Idea to IPO is a great way to find out what startups are trending and to get in early on the next big thing. You'll never know who you meet at the next event you attend.

Cost: TGIF Mixers are free, content events are $7 and up.

Link: http://www.idea-to-ipo.com

Social Media Managers (Facebook Group)

Where/When: Facebook group, events are usually not held

What: Social Media Managers is one of the largest Facebook groups focused on helping social media marketers succeed, excel, and stay up to date in their social media careers.

Why the Marketer Should Attend: Whether you intend to go the freelance route or the corporate journey, Social Media Managers has something for everyone. From conversations about how much a social media professional is worth to how to strategize on Snapchat, there's something to be learned daily. Those who want to learn on their own can also take advantage of Social Media Manager Pro, the product that sponsors the group.

Cost: Free

Link:
https://www.facebook.com/groups/socialmediamanagers/

SVForum

Where/When: Around the greater Silicon Valley region, events vary by days and are usually in the evenings

What: SVForum (Silicon Valley Forum), is the largest and oldest not-for-profit organization in Silicon Valley. They function as a center of knowledge and connections in Silicon Valley (from San Francisco to San Jose) - on anything from the latest tech trends to the startup and investment ecosystem. Now 30 years old, SV Forum focuses on and produce a variety of programs and projects based on the latest tech trends in Silicon Valley, as well as startup and investment-related topics such as: Next generation technology, enterprise software, digital media, green technology, health technology, and biotechnology (to name a few). They also cover startups and investments, tech women, diversity in technology, youth in technology, social good, and international programs.

Why the Marketer Should Attend: The startup scene is a special one in Silicon Valley and SVForum is at the heart. Marketers should attend to gain knowledge in related technologies, business strategies, and more. There may even be opportunities to work at startups from networking contacts at SVForum.

Cost: Varies per event.

Link: http://www.svforum.org/

Silicon Valley Young Professionals Network (YPN)

Where/When: Various locations throughout the South Bay on a monthly basis

What: SVYP is a group of young community and business leaders (aged 21-45) dedicated to improving the community by connecting and developing young professionals. SVYP focuses on providing networking and leadership opportunities in Santa Clara and Silicon Valley. SVYP programs include networking events, professional development programs and seminars, and quarterly social events designed to connect the up and coming leaders of Silicon Valley.

Why the Marketer Should Attend: Like its counterpart EPIC, SVYPN offers recent graduates an opportunity to discover a new network through a professional organization. Attendees and members will gain professional development skills, and those who are seeking jobs might find opportunities from other members who are at a similar skill and career level as them.

Cost: Varies per event

Link: http://www.siliconvalleyyp.com/

Closing Thoughts

I remember when I was a new graduate trying to make sense of the world I was handed. In the post-recession days of 2010, all of us were just beginning to see what uncertainty looked like.

It was these uncertainties that inspired me to start Albert's List about 3 years into my career. I realized though I was able to land on my feet, so many others were struggling. On our Facebook group, which now numbers in the tens of thousands, we have helped connect job seekers to a variety of employers including major name brands. Along the way, I've met a lot of great people doing great things, and learned to believe that most people just want an honest day's work.

If you're a new grad picking up this book for the very first time or re-reading it, I want you to know that you aren't alone in your struggle. The job hunt is a tough one and your pursuit of a great marketing career isn't easy especially when you are competing with hundreds of others for a single role. As long as you keep at the process of building your brand, networking, being transparent, and honing your skills, you will get what you deserve and the journey will be worth it. I know because I was once there myself.

As you reach the end of this book, I also want to invite you to continue the conversation. Every week on Albert's List we have job hunting tips, advice threads, job listings, opportunities to get involved, and opportunities to get involved. You'll find us at www.albertslist.org or reach out to us on our Twitter (@alberts_list) or our Facebook page.

Happy job hunting and networking!

Appendix: Networking Checklist

The following is a checklist to look at before attending any networking event. Best of luck, and have fun!

A Few Weeks Before the Event

◻ Research the event(s) you are interested in attending.
◻ Order business cards to hand out at the event. Suggested sites: http://www.moo.com, http://www.vistaprint.com
◻ Add event to your calendar. Invite friends to come along!

A Few Days Before the Event

◻ Check your calendar to make sure you can still attend.
◻ Research the event in advance. Ask your social network if anyone is going. You might meet up with someone you didn't expect!
◻ Schedule your work hours around the event, if necessary.

Day of the Event

◻ Check your calendar to make sure you can still attend.
◻ Make sure to have the right clothes for the event. Some events call for casual while other events want attendees to be a little bit more formal.
◻ Don't forget to put your business cards somewhere where you won't forget them! Have them handy and not in your wallet or back pocket.
◻ Make sure you know if there will be food or drink at the event. If not, ensure that you eat something before going.
◻ Print out your tickets.
◻ DO NOT: bring your resume. People do not want to see your resume -- they want to see you and what you are all about from a personal perspective.

▢ Get to the event on time -- make sure traffic is accounted for. Be aware of the parking situation, or take a Lyft or Uber.

At the Event

▢ Take a breath mint.

▢ DO: walk up and talk to other people. Some are at a networking event for the first time. Make them comfortable and feel at ease.

▢ DO: bring value to the conversation. Ask how you can help others, as opposed to what they do for a living.

▢ DO: spend time building relationships. However, get your money's worth too. You want to spend enough time on each conversation, but not too long.

▢ DO: listen, more than you speak.

▢ DO NOT: talk too much.

▢ DO NOT: just go to hand out business cards without the intention of building relationships with those you meet.

After the Event

▢ Thank the event organizer for putting it on. These things take hard work and a lot of effort.

▢ Follow up with every person who attended your event. Thank them for their time in speaking with you and suggest a follow up -- this can be coffee or a phone call. Add them on LinkedIn as well.

Appendix: Additional Resources and Reading

The following are some additional resources new graduates can use to maximize their networking opportunities in the Bay Area. Some may have already been mentioned in the area above. If you have additional ideas for what should be added, send an email to albert@albertslist.org.

Websites

- www.meetup.com - A fantastic resource for those looking for networking and social events. Hundreds of meetups happen every week and there is something for everyone.

- www.eventbrite.com - A fantastic website for event listings around the Bay Area. Eventbrite also has offices located in Downtown San Francisco.

- http://50waystogetajob.com/ - No matter where you are in your job search, you can always use new technology. This website helps you get there.

Business Cards

- www.moo.com - Offers unique business cards and postcard type collateral for new graduates to use.

- www.vistaprint.com - Offers free business cards though they take at least 3 weeks or more to arrive. Other stationery available for purchase as well.

Books

- *Fierce Conversations*, Susan Scott: Since you'll be having a lot of conversations around networking, this is a great book to pick up that will teach you how to approach each conversation with success.

- *Think and Grow Rich*, Napoleon Hill: This an oldie and a goodie. Long recommended by entrepreneurs, this book helps instill the mindset necessary to get on the grind of finding an employment opportunity.

- *The Four Agreements*, Don Miguel Ruiz: You'll no doubt run into conflicts when networking. *The Four Agreements* is a great read on what to take seriously and what to let go in times when everything seems like it matters.

- *Never Eat Alone,* Keith Ferrazi: In our lives we have many opportunities to break bread with others, but few of us take advantage. Recommended by power networkers, this book shows you how to get the most out of getting to know someone.

- *How to Win Friends and Influence People*, Dale Carnegie: Another oldie and goodie. Stephen Covey explains the philosophies that have endured over the past three-quarters of a century that have helped people become successful.

- *Choose Yourself*, James Altucher: With the economy at an all high-time high for uncertainty, serial entrepreneur James Altucher explains why you should choose yourself in the high stakes game of life, and how to succeed at doing so.

www.ingramcontent.com/pod-product-compliance
Lightning Source LLC
Chambersburg PA
CBHW070417190526
45169CB00003B/1291